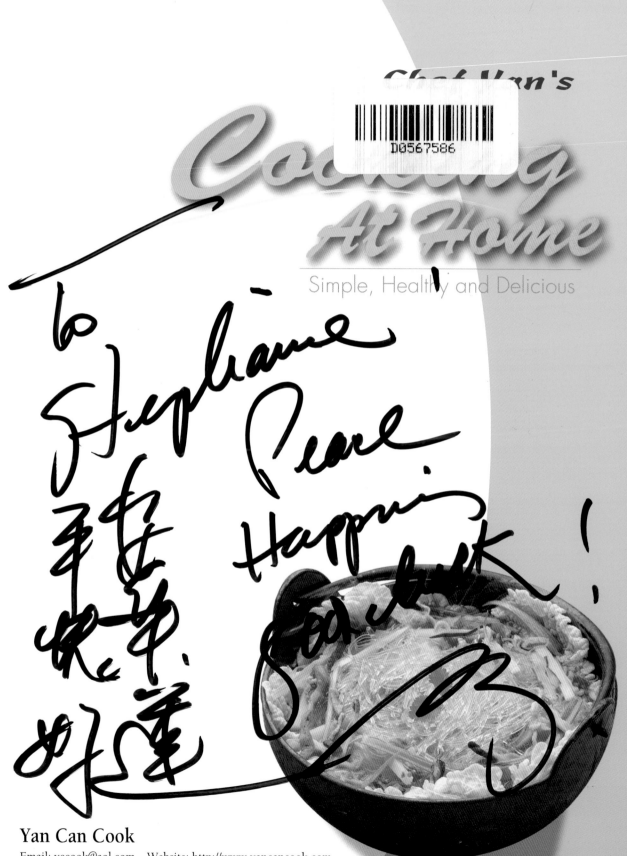

Chef Yan's
Cooking At Home
Simple, Healthy and Delicious

Yan Can Cook

Email: yccook@aol.com   Website: http://www.yancancook.com

Chef Yan's Cooking at Home

AUTHOR **Martin Yan**

PROJECT COORDINATOR FOR YAN CAN COOK **Stephanie Liu Jan**

FOOD PHOTOGRAPHY **Rosa To**

FOOD STYLIST **Stephanie Liu Jan**

PROP STYLIST **Stephanie Liu Jan** / **Rosa To**

FOOD PHOTOGRAPHY COORDINATOR **Stephanie Liu Jan**

PHOTOGRAPHY CHEFS **Mr. Frank Liou**

Helen Soehalim / **Vivienne Marsh** / **Anthony Tse** / **Julia Lee** /

Luke Fong

TRAVEL PHOTOGRAPHY **Stephanie Liu Jan**

EDITOR **Shek Kin**

DESIGNER **Lee Lai Ying** / **Wong Miu Ling**

First published in Hong Kong in 2000 by Wan Li Book Co., Ltd.

Unit 1, G/F, 5B-5F Ma Hang Chung Rd., Tokwawan, Kowloon, H.K.

TEL **2564 7511**   FAX **2565 5539**

WEBSITE **http://www.wanlibk.com**

ISBN 962-14-1795-3

Yan Can Cook, Inc.

P.O. Box 4755, Foster City, CA 94404, USA

Email: yccook@aol.com

Website: http://www.yancancook.com

Introduction

"If Yan can cook, so can you!" I've been saying that for years, and the message hasn't changed. It really is that simple.

Life on the road is not as glamorous as it sounds. Everybody pitches in to carry equipment and supplies. In the end, a good show makes all our hard work worthwhile. There is nothing like the strong support and positive feedback from our audience.

My philosophy of cooking and eating is pretty simple, too. You can sum it up in six words: Good food, good health, and good living. Over the years, I've consistently advocated eating healthfully without compromising flavor, convenience, or the joy of preparing and sharing food with others. This belief lies at the heart of the "Yan Can Cook" show, my books, and my other projects.

One of my long-term projects involves expanding global awareness and appreciation for Chinese and Asian food. I want to share our culinary treasures with the rest of the world, and I believe that the most effective way to do so is by bringing those cuisines and cultures to a hungry public in a lively, entertaining way. So, how am I doing so far?

Judging from the popularity of Asia's fabulous foods, and from your positive feedback — many thanks! — I'm not doing too shabby a job. And nothing makes me want to invite everyone to the Asian table more than your enthusiasm and support. So, I've collected recipes from many of my shows and classes to create this book for you. All of the dishes are easy to prepare, healthful, colorful, and, of course, delicious. They're great for comfy family meals at home as well as for those occasions when you really want to impress the guests.

The key to an exciting world of appetizing Chinese and Asian dishes is only a few easy recipe steps away. Fire up that wok and I'm sure you'll agree with what I've been telling you all along: You really can cook, too!

Martin Yan

CONTENTS

Tofu & Vegetables

Soups & Starches

Desserts

Glossary of Ingredients

Seafood in Lettuce Cups

◆ Marinade

½ egg white

1 teaspoon cornstarch

¼ teaspoon salt

⅛ teaspoon white pepper

¾ pound raw shrimp (shelled and deveined), scallops, or firm white fish fillet, such as sea bass or red snapper, coarsely chopped

◆ Seasonings

¼ cup chicken broth

2 teaspoons oyster-flavored sauce

½ teaspoon sesame oil

½ teaspoon cornstarch

¼ teaspoon sugar

2 tablespoons cooking oil

2 teaspoons minced garlic

½ onion, chopped

½ jalapeño or serrano chile, seeded and chopped

6 water chestnuts, chopped

2 tablespoons raisins

3 dried apricot halves, chopped

½ cup hoisin sauce

12 lettuce leaves, trimmed

◆ Method

1. Combine marinade ingredients in a bowl. Add seafood and stir to coat. Let stand for 10 minutes. Combine seasoning ingredients in a bowl; set aside.

2. Place a wok over high heat until hot. Add oil, swirling to coat sides. Add garlic, onion, and chile; cook, stirring, until fragrant, about 10 seconds. Add seafood, water chestnuts, raisins, and apricots; stir-fry for 1-½ minutes. Add seasonings and cook, stirring, until sauce boils and thickens. Remove to a serving platter.

3. To eat, spread a little hoisin sauce on a lettuce cup, spoon in some of seafood mixture, wrap up, and eat out of hand.

A cooking demonstration always captures the public's attention and is an effective way to generate international awareness of Asian cuisines and cultures.

Makes 4 to 6 servings

Sesame Seed Cakes

◆ Filling

10 dried black mushrooms

¾ cup chopped Sichuan preserved vegetable

2 pieces five-spice pressed bean curd, chopped

1 tablespoon chopped cooked ham

2 teaspoons sesame oil

1-½ teaspoons soy sauce

1-½ teaspoons sugar

5 tablespoons cooking oil

2 teaspoons cornstarch dissolved in 1 tablespoon water

◆ Batter

2 cups all-purpose flour

¼ teaspoon salt

2-¼ cups cold water

2 eggs, lightly beaten

1 tablespoon white sesame seeds

½ teaspoon black sesame seeds

1 egg, lightly beaten

◆ Method

1. Soak mushrooms in warm water to cover until softened, about 15 minutes; drain. Trim and discard stems. Chop caps.

2. Place mushrooms and preserved vegetable in a bowl. Add remaining filling ingredients and mix well.

3. Place a wok over medium heat until hot. Add 1 tablespoon oil, swirling to coat sides. Add filling and stir-fry for 3 minutes. Add cornstarch solution and cook, stirring, until mixture thickens. Remove filling to a bowl and let cool.

4. To make batter: Place flour and salt in a bowl; mix well. Add water, stirring constantly, until smooth. Add eggs and mix well. Pour batter through a sieve to remove lumps.

5. To make each pancake: Place a non-stick omelet pan over low heat until hot. Add ½ teaspoon oil, swirling to coat sides. Pour ⅓ cup batter into pan, swirling to form a thin layer. Cook until batter sets but is still moist on top. Sprinkle white and black sesame seeds over pancake. Turn pancake over and cook until lightly browned. Make two more pancakes with remaining batter and oil.

6. To make each cake: Place ⅓ cup filling across center of a pancake. Fold bottom of pancake over filling then fold in left and right sides. Roll up to form a loose cylinder; flatten slightly to form a rectangle. Brush with egg or flow paste to seal.

7. Place a wide frying pan over medium heat until hot. Add remaining 1 tablespoon oil, swirling to coat sides. Add filled cakes, half at a time. Cook, turning once, until golden brown, about 1-½ minutes on each side. Remove and drain on paper towels.

8. To serve, cut each cake in half and arrange on a serving platter.

Makes 4 to 6 servings

TIPS

To toast sesame seeds: Use a heavy-bottomed pan and toast seeds over low to medium-low heat. Shake pan often until seeds are lightly browned.

Chicken Salad

◆ Marinade

2 tablespoons rice wine or dry sherry

1 teaspoon minced garlic

½ pound boneless, skinless chicken

◆ Dressing

½ cup mayonnaise

2 tablespoons lemon juice

2 tablespoons sesame oil

1 teaspoon sugar

½ teaspoon salt

2 cups chicken broth

½ carrot, julienned

½ cucumber, seeded and julienned

½ head lettuce, shredded

¼ onion, thinly sliced

◆ Method

1. Combine marinade ingredients in a bowl. Add chicken and stir to coat. Let stand for 10 minutes. Combine dressing ingredients in a bowl; set aside.

2. Place broth in a saucepan and bring to a boil over high heat. Reduce heat to low. Add chicken and simmer, until chicken is cooked, about 10 to 12 minutes. Remove chicken to a bowl and let cool. Shred chicken and set aside.

3. Place carrot, cucumber, lettuce, and onion in a bowl; toss to combine. Place chicken on top. Pour dressing over salad and toss to coat. Remove to a serving platter and serve.

Makes 4 to 6 servings

TIPS

Partially freezing chicken hardens it. This makes it easier to cut chicken into paper-thin slices. Cut across the grain when finely shredding chicken to keep the shreds together during cooking.

Tofu Salad

◆ Sauce

⅓ cup chicken broth
2 tablespoons soy sauce
1 tablespoon rice vinegar
1 tablespoon sesame oil
2 teaspoons XO sauce (optional)
1 teaspoon chili garlic sauce
2 teaspoons sugar

1 tablespoon dried shrimp
1 tablespoon cooking oil
2 tablespoons coarsely chopped
   Sichuan preserved vegetable
1 teaspoon minced garlic
1 teaspoon minced ginger

1 green onion, sliced
½ teaspoon cornstarch dissolved in
   1 teaspoon water
1 package (16 ounces) soft tofu,
   drained

◆ Method

1. Combine sauce ingredients in a bowl; set aside.

2. Soak dried shrimp in warm water to cover for 5 minutes; drain. Coarsely chop shrimp and set aside.

3. Place a wok over high heat until hot. Add oil, swirling to coat sides. Add shrimp, preserved vegetable, garlic, ginger, and green onion; cook, stirring, until fragrant, about 10 seconds. Add sauce and cook until heated through. Add cornstarch solution and cook, stirring, until sauce boils and thickens.

4. To serve, cut tofu into 1-inch cubes and arrange in a shallow serving bowl. Pour sauce over tofu and serve.

Makes 4 to 6 servings

TIPS

If you've ever had the pleasure of dining at a traditional, upscale Hong Kong-style seafood restaurant patronized by gourmands of Chinese cuisine, you may have enjoyed a pungent condiment made from dried shrimp and scallops, red chile peppers, shrimp roe, shallots, garlic, and spices. Can you remember its name? It's not tough to recall: It's called XO sauce, and it's truly eXtraOrdinary. (How's that for a clue as to what its name means?) Developed by Hong Kong's gourmet chefs, it also goes by a more luxurious, but equally appropriate, nickname, "The Caviar of the Orient." Add a hint to sauces for noodles or short ribs and you'll be surprised at what flavors it awakens. I like to use it as a condiment with almost anything, or even as an appetizer by itself. It has caviar beaten by a long-shot.

Crispy Seafood Wraps

◆ Filling

½ pound firm white fish fillet, such as sea bass or red snapper, minced

3 ounces cream cheese, softened

½ cup minced crab meat

½ jalapeño or serrano chile, seeded and minced

2 tablespoons chopped cilantro

2 teaspoons soy sauce

1 teaspoon lemon juice

1 teaspoon sesame oil

¼ teaspoon white pepper

10 spring roll wrappers, cut into 8-inch by 2-½-inch pieces

1 tablespoon all-purpose flour dissolved in 2 tablespoons water

Cooking oil for deep-frying

◆ Method

1. Combine filling ingredients in a bowl and mix well.

2. To make each wrap: Place about one teaspoon filling at short end of a wrapper. Fold filling over to form a triangle. Continue folding, sealing last fold with flour paste.

3. Heat oil for deep-frying in a wok over medium-high heat until hot. Add half a dozen triangles and deep-fry, turning once, until golden brown, about 1-½ minutes on each side. Remove and drain on paper towels.

Makes 30 wraps

TIPS

Wonton, potsticker, and eggroll wrappers are all made with wheat flour, egg, and water. Dumplings and rolls made with these wrappers can be boiled, pan-fried, or deep-fried. Bean curd sheet, a product of soybean, will fall apart when boiled in water. Rolls made with bean curd sheet should only be pan-fried or deep-fried.

Kung Pao Fish

◆ Ingredients

¾ pound firm white fish fillets, such as sea bass or red snapper, each about ¾-inch thick

◆ Marinade

1 egg, lightly beaten
1 tablespoon soy sauce
2 teaspoons cornstarch
¼ teaspoon white pepper

◆ Seasonings

¼ cup chicken broth
2 tablespoons rice vinegar
1 tablespoon chili garlic sauce
2 teaspoons dark soy sauce
½ teaspoon sugar
¼ teaspoon salt

All-purpose flour for dusting
Cooking oil for deep-frying

4 dried red chiles
2 jalapeño or serrano chiles, seeded and cut into 1-inch pieces
2 teaspoons minced garlic
½ onion, cut into 1-inch pieces
1 green bell pepper, seeded and cut into diamond shapes
½ teaspoon cornstarch dissolved in 1 teaspoon water
¼ cup roasted peanuts

◆ Method

1. Cut fish into 1-½-inch pieces. Place fish in a bowl and add marinade ingredients; stir to coat. Let stand for 10 minutes. Combine seasoning ingredients in a bowl; set aside.

2. Dust fish with flour. Shake to remove excess. Heat oil for deep-frying in a wok over high heat until hot. Add fish and deep-fry, turning once, until golden brown, about 1-½ minutes on each side. Remove and drain on paper towels.

3. Remove all but 2 tablespoons oil from wok. Place wok over high heat until hot. Add dried and fresh chiles, garlic, onion, and bell pepper; stir-fry for 1 minute. Add fish and seasonings; cook until heated through. Add cornstarch solution and cook, stirring gently, until sauce boils and thickens. Remove to a serving platter and sprinkle peanuts over top.

Makes 4 to 6 servings

TIPS

"Kung Pao", a cooking style that originated in Sichuan, is characterized by the combination of sweet, sour, spicy and garlicky flavorings. Dried whole red chili peppers and roasted peanuts are always used in "Kung Pao" dishes.

Pan-fried Fish Fillet

◆ Ingredients

6 dried black mushrooms

2 ounces dried wood ears

1 pound firm white fish fillets, such as sea bass or red snapper, each about 1-inch thick

½ teaspoon salt

¼ teaspoon white pepper

◆ Sauce

⅓ cup chicken broth

2 tablespoons char siu sauce

2 tablespoons oyster-flavored sauce

1 tablespoon chili garlic sauce

1 tablespoon hoisin sauce or sweet bean paste

4 tablespoons cooking oil

6 slices ginger, lightly crushed

2 jalapeño or serrano chiles, seeded and sliced

2 green onions, cut into 2-inch pieces

◆ Method

1. Soak mushrooms in warm water to cover until softened, about 15 minutes; drain. Trim and discard stems. Thinly slice caps. Soak wood ears in warm water to cover until softened, about 5 minutes; drain. Thinly slice wood ears.

2. Cut fish into 2 pieces. Sprinkle salt and white pepper over fish. Let stand for 10 minutes. Combine sauce ingredients in a bowl; set aside.

3. Place a wok over high heat until hot. Add 2 tablespoons oil, swirling to coat sides. Add fish and cook, turning once, until golden brown, about 3 minutes on each side. Remove to a serving platter; keep warm.

4. Add remaining 2 tablespoons oil to wok, swirling to coat sides. Place wok over high heat until hot. Add ginger, chiles, and green onions; cook, stirring, until fragrant, about 10 seconds. Add mushrooms and wood ears; stir-fry for 1 minute. Add sauce and cook until heated through. Pour sauce over fish and serve.

TIPS

Barbecue sauce may conjure up images of cowboys roasting meats over an open flame, but the Chinese have their own version of this popular condiment, too. A mixture of fermented soy beans, vinegar, tomato paste, garlic, chiles, sugar, and other spices, Chinese barbecue sauce, called char siu sauce, is just as bold and hearty as its American counterpart. But with an aromatic character of its own, it's a far cry from the Old West, unless you're talking about China's Old West. Use it as a marinade, in sauces, or as a dipping or basting sauce. In fact, next time you mosey on over to a wild Western barbecue, bring along a little char siu sauce and taste what a difference it can make.

Makes 4 to 6 servings

Fish Fillet with Garlic Sauce

◆ Ingredients

1 pound salmon fillets, each about
¾-inch thick

◆ Marinade

1 slice ginger, julienned
2 cloves garlic, sliced
1 tablespoon soy sauce
½ teaspoon cornstarch
½ teaspoon salt
¼ teaspoon white pepper

◆ Sauce

¼ cup chicken broth
1 tablespoon rice wine or dry
sherry
2 teaspoons soy sauce
1 teaspoon black bean sauce
1 teaspoon sesame oil

3 tablespoons cooking oil
1 teaspoon minced garlic
1 teaspoon minced ginger
½ cup mayonnaise
Cilantro sprigs for garnish

◆ Method

1. Cut salmon into 3 pieces. Place salmon in a bowl and add marinade ingredients; turn to coat. Let stand for 10 minutes. Combine sauce ingredients in a bowl; set aside.

2. Place a wide frying pan over high heat until hot. Add 2 tablespoons oil, swirling to coat sides. Add salmon and pan-fry, turning once, until golden brown, about 2 minutes on each side. Remove to a serving platter; keep warm.

3. Add remaining 1 tablespoon oil to frying pan, swirling to coat sides. Place pan over medium heat until hot. Add garlic and ginger; cook, stirring, until fragrant, about 10 seconds. Add sauce and bring to a boil. Remove sauce to a bowl and let cool. Add mayonnaise and whisk until smooth. Serve salmon with sauce on the side. Garnish with cilantro sprigs.

There is always time for a quick game of chess between food shops.

Makes 4 to 6 servings

Stir-fried Squid

◆ Ingredients
¾ pound small squid, cleaned

◆ Marinade
1 tablespoon rice wine or dry sherry
2 teaspoons cornstarch
¼ teaspoon salt
¼ teaspoon white pepper

◆ Seasonings
3 tablespoons chicken broth
1 tablespoon rice wine or dry sherry
2 teaspoons sesame oil
1 teaspoon shrimp paste
¼ teaspoon sugar

2 tablespoons cooking oil

2 cloves garlic, sliced
2 slices ginger, julienned
2 tablespoons julienned cooked ham
8 green onions, cut into 2-inch pieces
½ teaspoon cornstarch dissolved in 1 teaspoon water

◆ Method
1. Separate squid tentacles from body. Slice open squid hoods and lightly score them diagonally with crosshatching marks ½ inch apart. Cut into 2-inch pieces. Leave tentacles whole.

2. Combine marinade ingredients in a bowl. Add squid and stir to coat. Let stand for 10 minutes. Combine seasoning ingredients in a bowl; set aside.

3. Place a wok over high heat until hot. Add oil, swirling to coat sides. Add garlic, ginger, and ham; cook, stirring, until fragrant, about 10 seconds. Add squid and stir-fry until squid begins to curl, 1 to 2 minutes. Add green onions and seasonings; bring to a boil. Add cornstarch solution and cook, stirring, until sauce boils and thickens.

TIPS

Music may soothe the savage beast, but a little cooking turns pungent, slightly fishy-smelling shrimp paste into a mellow, mildly salty, and almost indispensable flavoring ingredient in stir-fries, rice dishes, and savory braised casseroles. Made from salted fermented shrimp, the pinkish-gray sauce has an odor that reminds me of childhood fishing trips. The flavor gets my mind wandering, too–wandering right into the kitchen to stir up a little something with some shrimp paste.

Makes 4 to 6 servings

Chili Clams

◆**Ingredients**

1 pound small hard-shelled clams, well scrubbed

◆**Seasonings**

⅓ cup chicken broth

¼ cup ketchup

1 tablespoon chili garlic sauce

1 tablespoon soy sauce

1 tablespoon rice vinegar

2 teaspoons sugar

1 tablespoon cooking oil

2 teaspoons minced garlic

2 teaspoons minced ginger

Sliced green onion for garnish

◆**Method**

1. Bring a pot of water to a boil over high heat. Reduce heat to medium. Add clams and cook until clams begin to open, 2 to 3 minutes; drain. Discard any clams which do not open.

2. Combine seasoning ingredients in a bowl; set aside.

3. Place a wok over high heat until hot. Add oil, swirling to coat sides. Add garlic and ginger; cook, stirring, until fragrant, about 10 seconds. Add seasonings and bring to a boil. Add clams, cover, and cook until heated through, about 1 minute. Remove to a serving platter and garnish with green onion.

Makes 4 to 6 servings

TIPS

When purchasing clams, ensure their freshness by smelling them. Fresh clams do not smell "fishy". Gently squeeze the open shells of a clam together and let go; a fresh clam will keep its shells closed.

Prawns with Garlic Sauce

◆ Ingredients

¾ pound medium raw prawns in shell

¼ teaspoon salt

⅛ teaspoon white pepper

◆ Seasonings

¼ cup ketchup

¼ cup chicken broth

2 tablespoons dark soy sauce

2 teaspoons chili garlic sauce

1-½ teaspoons sugar

2 tablespoons cooking oil

2 teaspoons minced garlic

2 teaspoons minced ginger

1 jalapeño or serrano chili, seeded and chopped

1 green onion, chopped

2 teaspoons cornstarch dissolved in 1 tablespoon water

Toasted white sesame seeds for garnish

◆ Method

1. Remove prawn legs. If desired, cut through back of shells with scissors to remove sand vein. Combine salt and white pepper in a bowl. Add prawns and stir to coat. Let stand for 10 minutes. Combine seasoning ingredients in a bowl; set aside.

2. Place a wok over high heat until hot. Add 1 tablespoon oil, swirling to coat sides. Add prawns and stir-fry for 2 minutes. Remove prawns to a bowl and set aside.

3. Add remaining 1 tablespoon oil to wok, swirling to coat sides. Place wok over high heat until hot. Add garlic, ginger, chili, and green onion; cook, stirring, until fragrant, about 10 seconds. Return prawns to wok and add seasonings; bring to a boil. Reduce heat to low, cover, and simmer for 3 minutes. Add cornstarch solution and cook, stirring, until sauce boils and thickens. Remove to a serving platter and garnish with sesame seeds.

Makes 4 to 6 servings

TIPS

To devein shrimp with the shell on, use a toothpick to get between the second and third segments of the shrimp and remove the sandy vein.

Lychee Prawns

◆Ingredients
¾ pound medium raw prawns

◆Marinade
1 teaspoon cornstarch

¼ teaspoon salt

◆Seasonings
¼ cup prepared sweet and sour
  sauce

3 tablespoons chicken broth

1 teaspoon rice wine or dry sherry

1 teaspoon soy sauce

3 tablespoons cooking oil

3 jalapeño or serrano chiles, seeded
  and sliced

½ green bell pepper, seeded and cut
  into diamond shapes

¾ cup fresh or canned lychees,
  drained

◆Method
1. Shell and devein prawns.
   Butterfly prawns. Place in a bowl
   and add marinade ingredients;
   stir to coat. Let stand for 10
   minutes. Combine seasoning
   ingredients in a bowl; set aside.

2. Place a wok over high heat until
   hot. Add 2 tablespoons oil,
   swirling to coat sides. Add
   prawns and stir-fry for 1 to 2
   minutes. Remove prawns to a
   bowl and set aside.

3. Add remaining 1 tablespoon oil
   to wok, swirling to coat sides.
   Place wok over high heat until
   hot. Add chiles and bell pepper;
   cook, stirring, until fragrant,
   about 10 seconds. Return
   prawns to wok and add lychees
   and seasonings; cook until
   heated through.

Makes 4 to 6 servings

TIPS

Prolonged cooking of citrus fruits releases large amounts of citric acid from the fruits. Use only stainless steel pans because citric acid leeches out the metal from non-stainless steel pans. Citric acid also discolors chlorophyll in green vegetables and can make a dish taste sour. Citrus fruits should be added last and only cooked briefly to preserve the vitamins and fresh taste.

Scallops in Satay Sauce

◆ **Ingredients**

½ pound jumbo raw prawns

◆ **Marinade**

2 teaspoons rice wine or dry sherry

½ teaspoon cornstarch

¼ teaspoon salt

¼ teaspoon white pepper

½ pound sea scallops

1 teaspoon cornstarch

◆ **Seasonings**

¼ cup chicken broth

2 tablespoons soy sauce

4 teaspoons satay sauce

1-½ teaspoons sugar

3 tablespoons cooking oil

2 shallots, quartered

½ jalapeño or serrano chili, seeded and sliced

2 teaspoons minced garlic

2 green onions, cut into 2-inch pieces

1 teaspoon cornstarch dissolved in 2 teaspoons water

◆ **Method**

1. Shell and devein prawns. Butterfly prawns. Place in a bowl and add marinade ingredients; stir to coat. Let stand for 10 minutes.

2. Cut scallops in half horizontally. Place in a bowl and add cornstarch; stir to coat. Let stand for 10 minutes.

3. Bring a pot of water to a boil over high heat. Add scallops and cook until they just turn opaque, about 1-½ minutes; drain.

4. Combine seasoning ingredients in a bowl; set aside.

5. Place a wok over high heat until hot. Add 2 tablespoons oil, swirling to coat sides. Add prawns and scallops; stir-fry for 2 minutes. Remove seafood to a bowl and set aside.

6. Add remaining 1 tablespoon oil to wok, swirling to coat sides. Place wok over high heat until hot. Add shallots, chili, and garlic; cook, stirring, until fragrant, about 10 seconds. Add seasonings and cook until heated through. Return seafood to wok and add green onions; cook for 1 minute. Add cornstarch solution and cook, stirring, until sauce boils and thickens.

Makes 4 to 6 servings

TIPS

Satay sauce is hot-in more ways than one! This classic peanut sauce, which hails from the area around Indonesia, Malaysia, and Singapore has become popular lately, thanks to its rich, spicy-sweet flavor and taste-tempting effect on everything from barbecued skewered meats to noodle and stir-fried dishes. Although ground peanuts play the starring role in satay sauce, chiles, garlic, ginger, palm sugar, soy sauce, sesame oil, and shallots–among other ingredients-help round out the cast and create an irresistibly complex flavor.

Crispy Seafood Triangles

◆ Ingredients

¼ pound medium raw prawns, shelled, deveined, and finely chopped

¼ pound bay scallops, chopped

¼ pound firm white fish fillets, such as sea bass or red snapper, chopped

◆ Marinade

1 egg white, lightly beaten

2 tablespoons chopped cilantro

2 tablespoons oyster-flavored sauce

1 tablespoon XO sauce (optional)

1 tablespoon rice wine or dry sherry

2 teaspoons sesame oil

1 teaspoon ginger juice

1 tablespoon cornstarch

6 tablespoons cooking oil

⅓ cup finely diced jicama

8 pieces bean curd sheets, each 10-inches by 5-inches

2 green onions, chopped

1 tablespoon all-purpose flour dissolved in 2 tablespoons water

Worcestershire sauce for dipping

◆ Method

1. Combine prawns, scallops, and fish in a bowl. Add marinade ingredients and mix well. Let stand for 10 minutes.

2. Place a wok over high heat until hot. Add 2 tablespoons oil, swirling to coat sides. Add seafood and stir-fry for 2 minutes. Add jicama and cook for 1 minute. Remove seafood mixture to a bowl and let cool.

3. To make each triangle: Place ¼ cup seafood mixture along short end of bean curd sheet. Sprinkle green onions over seafood mixture. Fold filling over to form a triangle. Continue folding, sealing last fold with flour paste.

4. Place a wide frying pan over high heat until hot. Add 2 tablespoons oil, swirling to coat sides. Add half the triangles and pan-fry, turning once, until golden brown, about 2 minutes on each side. Remove and drain on paper towels. Cook remaining triangles with remaining oil.

5. Arrange on a serving platter and serve with Worcestershire sauce on the side for dipping.

Makes 10 to 12

32

Seafood and Eggplant Stir-fry

◆ Ingredients

¼ pound small raw prawns

¼ pound small squid, cleaned

¼ pound sea scallops

◆ Marinade

2 tablespoons rice wine or dry sherry

1 tablespoon cornstarch

½ teaspoon salt

⅛ teaspoon white pepper

◆ Seasonings

¾ cup chicken broth

1 tablespoon hoisin sauce

1 tablespoon rice vinegar

1 tablespoon soy sauce

1 teaspoon sesame oil

1 teaspoon packed brown sugar

Cooking oil for deep-frying

¾ pound Asian eggplants, roll-cut

1 teaspoon minced garlic

1 tablespoon chopped Sichuan preserved vegetable

3 green onions, cut into 1-½-inch pieces

◆ Method

1. Shell and devein prawns. Separate squid tentacles from body. Cut hood into rings; leave tentacles whole. Cut scallops in half horizontally. Place scallops, prawns, and squid in a bowl. Add marinade ingredients and stir to coat. Let stand for 10 minutes. Combine seasoning ingredients in a bowl; set aside.

2. Heat oil for deep-frying in a wok over medium heat until hot. Add eggplants and deep-fry until golden brown, about 2 minutes. Remove and drain on paper towels.

3. Remove all but 2 tablespoons oil from wok. Place wok over high heat until hot. Add garlic and cook, stirring, until fragrant, about 10 seconds. Add seafood mixture and stir-fry for 1 minute. Add eggplants, preserved vegetable, green onions, and seasonings; bring to a boil. Reduce heat to low and simmer for 2 minutes.

Makes 4 to 6 servings

Whenever possible, I go to the park for some morning Tai Chi—nothing like a little exercise to stimulate my appetite!!

Hot and Sour Crab

◆Ingredients

1 live Dungeness crab, cleaned

◆Sauce

⅓ cup chicken broth

2 tablespoons rice vinegar

1 teaspoon chili garlic sauce

1 teaspoon chopped mint

2 teaspoons sugar

¼ teaspoon salt

2 tablespoons cooking oil

2 teaspoons minced garlic

2 teaspoons minced ginger

1 green onion, thinly sliced diagonally

1 jalapeño or serrano chili, seeded and chopped

◆Method

1. Bring a pot of water to a boil over high heat. Add crab and parboil for 2 minutes. Drain, rinse with cold water, and drain again. Pull off the top shell in one piece and discard. Remove and discard gills and spongy parts under the shell. Twist off claws and legs; crack with a cleaver or mallet. Cut body into 6 pieces. Place crab in a bowl, cover, and refrigerate until chilled.

2. Combine sauce ingredients in a bowl; set aside.

3. Place a wok over high heat until hot. Add oil, swirling to coat sides. Add garlic, ginger, green onion, and chili; cook, stirring, until fragrant, about 10 seconds. Add sauce and bring to a boil. Remove sauce to a bowl and let cool.

4. Arrange crab in a shallow serving bowl and serve with sauce on the side for dipping.

Makes 4 to 6 servings

TIPS

Crabs are delicious and wonderful foods. However, they are high in cholesterol, and should only be eaten in moderation. In Chinese cooking, crabs are Yin foods, and are often eaten with ginger and vinegar, Yang foods, for balance.

Double Happiness Prawns

◆ Seasonings

1 tablespoon chicken broth
2 teaspoons orange liqueur, such as Cointreau
½ teaspoon sesame oil
2 teaspoons cornstarch
¼ teaspoon salt
¼ teaspoon sugar
¼ teaspoon white pepper

1 pound large raw prawns
All-purpose flour for dusting
2 green apples
2 slices cooked ham, about ⅛-inch thick
2 tablespoons cooking oil
1 teaspoon minced garlic
1 teaspoon minced ginger

◆ Method

1. Combine seasoning ingredients in a bowl; set aside.

2. Shell and devein prawns. Butterfly prawns then make a second slit through the middle. Dust prawns with flour. Shake to remove excess.

3. Peel and core apples. Cut apples in half and thinly slice. Slice ham to a size that matches apple slices.

4. To make each prawn: Place a ham slice between two apple slices. Place ham and apple through slit in prawn.

5. Place a wok over high heat until hot. Add oil, swirling to coat sides. Add prawns and cook until prawns turn pink and curl slightly, about 3 minutes. Remove prawns to a bowl and set aside.

6. Add garlic and ginger; cook, stirring, until fragrant, about 10 seconds. Return prawns to wok and add seasonings; cook until heated through.

Makes 4 to 6 servings

Savory Purses

◆ Marinade

1 tablespoon cornstarch
1 tablespoon soy sauce
1 teaspoon sugar

¾ pound boneless, skinless chicken breast, coarsely chopped
6 dried black mushrooms

◆ Seasonings

1 tablespoon soy sauce
1 tablespoon oyster-flavored sauce
1 tablespoon rice wine or dry sherry
2 teaspoons sesame oil
2 teaspoons cornstarch
1 teaspoon sugar

2 tablespoons cooking oil

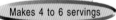
Makes 4 to 6 servings

2 teaspoons minced garlic
2 jalapeño or serrano chiles, thinly sliced
1 onion, thinly sliced
6 water chestnuts, diced
1 carrot, julienned
12 crepes
12 cilantro sprigs
12 green onion strips

◆ Method

1. Combine marinade ingredients in a bowl. Add chicken and stir to coat. Cover and refrigerate for 30 minutes.

2. Soak mushrooms in warm water to cover until softened, about 15 minutes; drain. Trim and discard stems. Thinly slice caps. Combine seasoning ingredients in a bowl; set aside.

3. Place a wok over medium heat until hot. Add oil, swirling to coat sides. Add garlic, chiles, and onion; cook, stirring, until onion becomes translucent, about 2 minutes. Add chicken, mushrooms, water chestnuts, and carrot; stir-fry for 2 minutes. Add seasonings and cook until heated through. Remove chicken mixture to a bowl.

4. To make each purse: Place 2 tablespoons chicken mixture in center of a crepe. Place a cilantro sprig on top. Gather edges of crepe over filling and tie with a green onion strip.

Crepes

◆ Ingredients

2 eggs
2-½ cups whole milk
2 tablespoons cooking oil
⅛ teaspoon salt
2 cups all-purpose flour
¼ cup butter

◆ Method

1. Beat eggs in a bowl until frothy.

Makes 12 crepes

Add milk, oil, and salt; beat after each addition. Gradually add flour; beat after each addition until smooth. Cover and let stand for 20 minutes.

2. To make each crepe: Place a non-stick omelet pan over medium heat until hot. Add a teaspoon of butter, swirling to

coat sides. Pour ¼ cup batter into pan, swirling to coat sides. Cook until golden brown and crepe starts to loosen from pan when shaken. Turn over and cook until golden brown. Remove to a serving platter. Prepare about 11 more crepes with remaining batter and butter.

Mu Shu Chicken

◆ Ingredients

6 dried black mushrooms

½ pound boneless, skinless chicken

◆ Marinade

1 tablespoon soy sauce

1 tablespoon rice wine or dry sherry

1 teaspoon cornstarch

◆ Seasonings

¼ cup chicken broth

2 tablespoons hoisin sauce

2 tablespoons soy sauce

1 teaspoon sesame oil

2 tablespoons chicken broth

¼ pound asparagus, thinly sliced diagonally

2 tablespoons cooking oil

2 teaspoons minced ginger

½ onion, thinly sliced

½ teaspoon cornstarch dissolved in 1 teaspoon water

12 mu shu wrappers or spring roll wrappers

◆ Method

1. Soak mushrooms in warm water to cover until softened, about 15 minutes; drain. Trim and discard stems. Thinly slice caps.

2. Thinly slice chicken then cut slices into thin strips. Remove to a bowl and add marinade ingredients; stir to coat. Let stand for 10 minutes. Combine seasoning ingredients in a bowl; set aside.

3. Place broth in a saucepan and bring to a boil over high heat. Add asparagus and cook until tender-crisp, about 1 minute; drain.

4. Place a wok over high heat until hot. Add oil, swirling to coat sides. Add ginger and onion; cook, stirring, until fragrant, about 10 seconds. Add chicken and mushrooms; stir-fry for 2 minutes. Add asparagus and seasonings; cook for 1 minute. Add cornstarch solution and cook, stirring, until sauce boils and thickens.

5. To serve, place ⅓ cup chicken mixture along center of a mu shu wrapper. Fold short end over filling then fold in sides.

TIPS

In Sichuan dialect, "Mu Shu" refers to "everything shredded". Any meat or vegetable can be shredded, and stir-fried to make a "Mu Shu" dish.

Makes 4 to 6 servings

Sweet and Sour Chicken

◆ **Marinade**

2 teaspoons soy sauce

1 teaspoon rice wine or dry sherry

½ teaspoon cornstarch

½ pound boneless, skinless chicken, cut into ¾-inch pieces

◆ **Seasonings**

¼ cup prepared sweet and sour sauce

2 tablespoons rice vinegar

1 tablespoon tomato paste

2 teaspoons soy sauce

1 teaspoon salt

½ teaspoon sugar

3 tablespoons cooking oil

2 slices ginger, lightly crushed

2 green onions, cut into 1-inch pieces

1 jalapeño or serrano chili, seeded and sliced

1 apple, peeled, seeded, and cut into cubes

1 mango, peeled, seeded, and cut into cubes

½ Asian pear, peeled, cored, and cut into cubes

½ cup diced pineapple

◆ **Method**

1. Combine marinade ingredients in a bowl. Add chicken and stir to coat. Let stand for 10 minutes. Combine seasoning ingredients in a bowl; set aside.

2. Place a wok over high heat until hot. Add 2 tablespoons oil, swirling to coat sides. Add chicken and stir-fry for 2 minutes. Remove chicken to a bowl and set aside.

3. Add remaining 1 tablespoon oil to wok, swirling to coat sides. Place wok over high heat until hot. Add ginger, green onions, and chili; cook, stirring, until fragrant, about 10 seconds. Add apple, mango, Asian pear, pineapple, and seasonings; cook for 1 minute. Return chicken to wok and cook until heated through.

Makes 4 to 6 servings

TIPS

In different recipes, various sizes and shapes of meats are called for. This is usually dictated by the cooking method and cooking time. No matter what size is called for, make sure the meat is cut to the same size and shape as the other ingredients in the dish. This way, the cooking time can be better controlled, the meat will cook more evenly, and the finished dish will look nicer.

Chicken with Gingko Nuts

◆ Marinade

1 tablespoon soy sauce
1 teaspoon cornstarch
¼ teaspoon salt
⅛ teaspoon white pepper

½ pound boneless, skinless chicken, cut into ¾-inch pieces
3 dried black mushrooms

◆ Seasonings

3 tablespoons chicken broth
1 tablespoon soy sauce
1 teaspoon hoisin sauce
1 teaspoon rice wine or dry sherry
1 teaspoon sesame oil
½ teaspoon sugar

Cooking oil for deep-frying
¼ pound canned gingko nuts, drained (optional)

3 tablespoons whole blanched almonds
1 small green bell pepper, seeded and cut into diamond shapes
1 small red bell pepper, seeded and cut into diamond shapes

◆ Method

1. Combine marinade ingredients in a bowl. Add chicken and stir to coat. Let stand for 10 minutes. Soak mushrooms in warm water to cover until softened, about 15 minutes; drain. Trim and discard stems. Cut caps into quarters. Combine seasoning ingredients in a bowl; set aside.

2. Heat oil for deep-frying in a wok over high heat. Add gingko nuts and deep-fry until golden brown, about 1 minute. Remove and drain on paper towels. Add almonds and deep-fry until golden brown, about 2 minutes. Remove and drain on paper towels.

3. Remove all but 2 tablespoons oil from wok. Place wok over high heat until hot. Add chicken and mushrooms; stir-fry for 2 minutes. Add green and red bell peppers and gingko nuts; cook for 1 minute. Add seasonings and cook until heated through. Remove to a serving platter and garnish with almonds.

Makes 4 to 6 servings

TIPS

Thanks to studies showing that the *Ginkgo biloba* plant may help boost brain function, this ancient Asian tree and its byproducts have earned quite a following among folks eager for a mental "edge." But the Chinese have turned to the ginkgo for years, and for much tastier reasons. Its seeds are buff-colored, mildly sweet nuts that work equally well in desserts and in savory dishes such as this. If you live near an Asian market, you may find fresh ginkgo nuts in fall and winter, but you can find dried or canned versions year-round.

Chicken with Lemon Sauce

◆ Ingredients

¾ pound boneless, skinless chicken

◆ Marinade

1-½ tablespoons soy sauce
2 teaspoons cornstarch
½ teaspoon salt
½ teaspoon sugar
⅛ teaspoon white pepper

◆ Sauce

1 teaspoon grated lemon peel
1 teaspoon minced ginger
⅓ cup chicken broth
⅓ cup lemon juice
1 tablespoon sugar

2 tablespoons cooking oil
1 teaspoon cornstarch dissolved in
2 teaspoons water

◆ Method

1. Cut chicken into 1-½-inch pieces; lightly pound to flatten. Place in a bowl and add marinade ingredients; stir to coat. Let stand for 10 minutes. Combine sauce ingredients in a saucepan; set aside.

2. Place a wide frying pan over medium heat until hot. Add oil, swirling to coat sides. Add chicken and pan-fry, turning once, until golden brown, about 2 minutes on each side. Remove chicken to a serving platter.

3. Bring sauce to a boil over medium heat. Add cornstarch solution and cook, stirring, until sauce boils and thickens. Pour sauce over chicken and serve.

I'll never forget the simple pleasures of cooking in my grandmother's traditional kitchen in the Chinese countryside. In fact, I got a chance to do just that when visiting her during the filming of my series.

Makes 4 to 6 servings

Braised Chicken with Chestnuts

◆ Ingredients

2 ounces fresh or dried chestnuts

¾ pound boneless chicken

◆ Marinade

1 tablespoon soy sauce

½ teaspoon sesame oil

1 teaspoon cornstarch

◆ Seasonings

1-½ cups chicken broth

1 tablespoon oyster-flavored sauce

1 tablespoon dark soy sauce

1 teaspoon sesame oil

⅔ pound taro root

Cooking oil for deep-frying

3 cloves garlic, lightly crushed

◆ Method

1. Remove shells from fresh chestnuts. Bring a saucepan of water to a boil over medium heat. Add fresh chestnuts; cover and cook until chestnuts begin to soften, about 5 minutes. If dried chestnuts are used, bring a saucepan of water to a boil over medium heat. Add dried chestnuts, cover, and cook until chestnuts begin to soften, about 30 minutes. Drain and set aside. Drain and set aside.

2. Cut chicken into ¾-inch pieces. Place in a bowl and add marinade ingredients; stir to coat. Let stand for 10 minutes. Combine seasoning ingredients in a bowl; set aside.

3. Peel taro root and cut into 1-inch pieces. Heat oil for deep-frying in a wok over high heat until hot. Reduce heat to medium-high. Add taro root and deep-fry until golden brown, about 5 minutes. Remove and drain on paper towels.

4. Remove all but 2 tablespoons oil from wok. Place wok over high heat until hot. Add garlic and cook, stirring, until fragrant, about 10 seconds. Add chicken; stir-fry for 1 minute. Add chestnuts, taro root, and seasonings; bring to a boil. Reduce heat to low, cover, and simmer until taro root is tender, 10 - 12 minutes.

Note: If taro root is not available, you can substitute potatoes.

Makes 6 servings

TIPS

Chestnuts are abundant and harvested in August and September. The best method to preserve chestnuts is by air-drying because sun-drying destroys the sugars in the chestnuts. Soak the dried chestnuts overnight in warm water before using in a recipe.

Sometimes your hands may itch when you are preparing taro. Wash hands with a little vinegar, then dry them over a warm burner. This calms the itch. The same method can be used to soothe the burning feeling when touching chili peppers. Salt may be used instead of vinegar.

Mongolian Lamb

◆ Marinade

1 tablespoon soy sauce

¼ teaspoon cornstarch

¾ pound boneless lamb, thinly sliced

◆ Seasonings

2 tablespoons hoisin sauce

1 tablespoon white vinegar

1 tablespoon soy sauce

1 teaspoon sesame oil

2 teaspoons sugar

2-½ tablespoons cooking oil

4 cloves garlic, sliced

½ onion, sliced

4 green onions, cut into 1-½-inch pieces

½ green bell pepper, seeded and cut into diamond shapes

½ red bell pepper, seeded and cut into diamond shapes

½ teaspoon cornstarch dissolved in 1 teaspoon water

Coarsely chopped cilantro for garnish

◆ Method

1. Combine marinade ingredients in a bowl. Add lamb and stir to coat. Let stand for 10 minutes. Combine seasoning ingredients in a bowl; set aside.

2. Place a wok over high heat until hot. Add 2 tablespoons oil, swirling to coat sides. Add garlic and cook, stirring, until fragrant, about 10 seconds. Add lamb and stir-fry until barely pink, about 1 minute. Remove lamb to a bowl and set aside.

3. Add remaining ½ tablespoon oil to wok, swirling to coat sides. Place wok over high heat until hot. Add onion and green onions; cook, stirring, until fragrant, about 10 seconds. Add green and red bell peppers; stir-fry for 30 seconds. Add seasonings and bring to a boil. Add cornstarch solution and cook, stirring, until sauce boils and thickens. Return lamb to wok and toss to coat. Remove to a serving platter and sprinkle cilantro on top.

I've come all the way to the Great Wall in my authentic Mongolian soldier's uniform for some authentic Mongolian lamb. But with this recipe—easy to conquer even for this poorly trained soldier—you don't need to travel nearly so far.

Makes 4 to 6 servings

Beef and Vegetable Rolls

◆ Ingredients
½ pound New York steak

◆ Marinade
2 teaspoons chopped ginger
2 tablespoons soy sauce
1 tablespoon cooking oil
⅛ teaspoon white pepper

5 dried black mushrooms

◆ Seasonings
1 tablespoon soy sauce
1 teaspoon sesame oil
¼ teaspoon sugar

◆ Sauce
¼ cup chicken broth
1 tablespoon oyster-flavored sauce
1 tablespoon rice wine or dry sherry
¼ teaspoon sugar
⅛ teaspoon white pepper

2 tablespoons cooking oil
1 onion, thinly sliced
1 green onion, cut into 2-inch pieces
½ red bell pepper, seeded and julienned

¼ pound enoki mushrooms, trimmed
2 tablespoons butter
½ teaspoon cornstarch dissolved in 1 teaspoon water

◆ Method
1. Partially freeze steak for 30 minutes or until firm to facilitate slicing. Cut steak horizontally across the grain into 4-inch by 2-inch by ⅛-inch slices. Lightly pound to flatten. Place in a bowl and add marinade ingredients; stir to coat. Let stand for 10 minutes.

2. Soak mushrooms in warm water to cover until softened, about 15 minutes; drain. Trim and discard stems. Thinly slice caps. Combine seasoning ingredients in a bowl; set aside. Combine sauce ingredients in a saucepan; set aside.

3. Place a wok over high heat until hot. Add oil, swirling to coat sides. Add onion, green onion, bell pepper, and black mushrooms; stir-fry for 30 seconds. Add enoki mushrooms and seasonings; cook for 1 minute. Remove vegetable mixture to a bowl and let cool.

4. To make each roll: Place 2 tablespoons vegetable mixture across short end of a piece of steak. Roll up and secure with a toothpick.

5. Place a wide frying pan over medium-high heat until hot. Add butter, swirling to coat sides. Add beef rolls and pan-fry until browned on all sides, about 2 minutes. Arrange beef rolls on a serving platter.

6. Bring sauce to a boil over medium heat. Add cornstarch solution and cook, stirring, until sauce boils and thickens. Pour sauce over beef rolls and serve.

Makes 4 to 6 servings

Mandarin Beef Steak

◆ Ingredients
1 pound beef tenderloin

◆ Marinade
2 tablespoons soy sauce

1 tablespoon rice wine or dry sherry

1 tablespoon cornstarch

◆ Seasonings
¼ cup chicken broth

2 tablespoons hoisin sauce

2 tablespoons ketchup

1 tablespoon soy sauce

1 tablespoon Worcestershire sauce

2 teaspoons cornstarch

2 tablespoons cooking oil

2 tablespoons butter

1 onion, thinly sliced

2 tablespoons white vinegar

2 teaspoons packed brown sugar

1 red bell pepper, seeded and thinly sliced

◆ Method

1. Cut beef into 2-½-inch pieces about ½-inch thick. Place beef in a bowl and add marinade ingredients; stir to coat. Let stand for 10 minutes. Combine seasoning ingredients in a bowl; set aside.

2. Place a wide frying pan over high heat until hot. Add 2 tablespoons oil, swirling to coat sides. Add beef and pan-fry until barely pink, about 2 minutes. Remove beef to a bowl and set aside.

3. Place pan over medium-high heat. Add butter, swirling to coat sides. Add onion and cook, stirring, until onion becomes translucent, about 2 minutes. Add vinegar and brown sugar; cook, stirring, until onion is caramelized, about 1 minute. Remove to a serving platter.

4. Add bell pepper and stir-fry for 30 seconds. Return beef to wok and add seasonings; cook until heated through. Pour beef and bell peppers over onions and serve.

Makes 4 to 6 servings

Oxtail in Red Wine Sauce

◆ Ingredients

2-¼ pounds oxtail, cut into segments

◆ Seasonings

2 tablespoons dark soy sauce

2 tablespoons oyster-flavored sauce

1 tablespoon rock sugar

1 stick cinnamon

1 teaspoon sugar

2 tablespoons cooking oil

6 slices ginger, lightly crushed

4 cloves garlic, lightly crushed

3 shallots, quartered and lightly crushed

1 stalk lemongrass (bottom 6 inches only), thinly sliced

5 cups water

½ cup red wine

½ pound daikon, roll-cut

1 small carrot, roll-cut

2 green onions, cut into 2-inch pieces

4 teaspoons cornstarch dissolved in 3 tablespoons water

◆ Method

1. Bring a pot of water to a boil over high heat. Add oxtail and parboil for 5 minutes. Pour into a colander and let drain. Combine seasoning ingredients in a bowl; set aside.

2. Place a pot over high heat until hot. Add oil, swirling to coat sides. Add ginger, garlic, shallots, and lemongrass; cook, stirring, until fragrant, about 10 seconds. Add water and red wine; bring to a boil. Add oxtail and seasonings; bring to a boil. Reduce heat to low, cover, and simmer for 2 hours. Add daikon and carrot; cook until vegetables are tender when pierced, about 30 minutes. Add green onions and cook for 30 seconds. Add cornstarch solution and cook, stirring, until sauce boils and thickens.

I'm visiting a famous Shao Hsing wine factory while filming my series. These huge jars—the Chinese version of wine barrels—are just about the right size for storing all the wine that adds such delicious flavor to Chinese dishes.

TIPS

How sweet it is! Well, not too sweet-at least, not when you're using rock sugar, which is the sugar to use when creating a smooth, mellow sweetness in a savory braised dish or a sauce. This pale, amber-colored crystal, also known as rock candy, is a combination of refined and unrefined sugars. Thus, it has none of the cloying sweetness of refined white sugar, which makes it perfect for those dishes that come before dessert. You can find rock sugar in plastic packages and cellophane-wrapped boxes in Asian markets. If stored in a tightly sealed container in a cool, dry place, it will keep for several months.

Makes 4 to 6 servings

Black Pepper Beef

◆ Marinade

2 tablespoons soy sauce
1 tablespoon rice wine or dry sherry
1 teaspoon cornstarch

¾ pound flank steak, thinly sliced

◆ Seasonings

¼ cup chicken broth
2 teaspoons dark soy sauce
2 teaspoons sesame oil
2 teaspoons hoisin sauce
1 teaspoon sugar
½ teaspoon black pepper

3 tablespoons cooking oil
2 slices ginger, julienned

2 teaspoons minced garlic
1 jalapeño or serrano chili, seeded and julienned
½ carrot, julienned
¼ pound garlic chives, cut into 1-½-inch pieces
1 green onion, julienned

◆ Method

1. Combine marinade ingredients in a bowl. Add beef and stir to coat. Let stand for 10 minutes. Combine seasoning ingredients in a bowl; set aside.

2. Place a wok over high heat until hot. Add 2 tablespoons oil, swirling to coat sides. Add ginger, garlic, and chili; cook, stirring, until fragrant, about 10 seconds. Add beef and stir-fry until barely pink, about 1-½ minutes. Remove beef to a bowl and set aside.

3. Add remaining 1 tablespoon oil to wok, swirling to coat sides. Place wok over high heat until hot. Add carrot, garlic chives, and green onion; stir-fry for 1 minute. Return beef to wok and add seasonings; cook until heated through.

Visiting a neighborhood street market is both fun and educational. I can't think of a better way to explore the local cuisine.

Makes 4 to 6 servings

Hainanese Lamb Stew

◆ Ingredients

8 Chinese red dates
2 pieces dried wood ears
1 ounce dried longan
2 tablespoons wolfberries
1 pound boneless lamb
¼ pound daikon

◆ Seasonings

2 tablespoons soy sauce
1 tablespoon dark soy sauce
1 teaspoon chili garlic sauce
1 teaspoon salt
1 teaspoon sugar

Cooking oil for deep-frying
1 dried bean curd stick
2 slices ginger, lightly crushed
¼ cup red wine
1-½ cups water
6 mint leaves

◆ Method

1. Place red dates, wood ears, longan, and wolfberries in separate bowls and soak in warm water to cover until softened, about 15 minutes; drain. Tear wood ear into bite-size pieces.

2. Cut lamb into 1-½-inch pieces. Peel daikon and cut into ½-inch cubes.

3. Bring a pot of water to a boil. Add lamb and parboil for 1-½ minutes. Pour into a colander and let drain. Combine seasoning ingredients in a bowl; set aside.

4. Heat oil for deep-frying in a wok over high heat until hot. Add bean curd stick and deep-fry until golden brown, about 30 seconds. Remove and drain on paper towels. Break into 2-inch pieces.

5. Remove all but 1 tablespoon oil from wok. Place wok over high heat until hot. Add ginger and cook, stirring, until fragrant, about 10 seconds. Add lamb and cook for 1-½ minutes. Add red dates, wood ears, longan, wolfberries, daikon, bean curd stick, red wine, and water; bring to a boil. Reduce heat to low, cover, and simmer for 40 minutes.

6. Add seasoning ingredients and mint leaves; cook for another 20 minutes.

Makes 4 to 6 servings

TIPS

Dried fruits make great snacks and bring a pleasant texture contrast and tart-sweet flavor to braised dishes such as this lamb casserole. But many Chinese dried fruits-wolfberries and Chinese red dates among them-also have reported medicinal benefits. Wolfberries, the small, bright red fruits of the medlar tree, have a wrinkled, chewy texture when dried and an intriguing flavor often compared to that of spiced apples. As if that weren't enough, they supposedly act as tonics for the kidneys and lungs. (Cranberries make tasty substitutes and have long been used to treat kidney infections, to boot.) Chinese red dates, also known as jujubes, are small, wrinkled fruits (unrelated to the palm date) with a tangy-sweet flavor also reminiscent of apples. Not only are they enjoyed for their sweet taste when candied or in glutinous rice puddings and stews, but they may also help alleviate anxiety. Just thinking about them makes me feel calm–and hungry.

Savory Stuffed Mushrooms

◆ Filling

½ pound medium raw prawns

8 water chestnuts, minced

1 tablespoon dried shrimp, soaked and minced

1 tablespoon minced ginger

2 teaspoons chopped cilantro

◆ Marinade

1 egg white, lightly beaten

1 tablespoon soy sauce

2 teaspoons rice wine or dry sherry

1 teaspoon cornstarch

½ teaspoon salt

¼ teaspoon sugar

¼ teaspoon white pepper

12 large white button mushrooms

Cornstarch for dusting

2 tablespoons cooking oil

◆ Method

1. To prepare filling: Shell and devein prawns. Mince prawns and place in a bowl. Add remaining filling ingredients and mix well. Add marinade ingredients and mix well. Let stand for 10 minutes.

2. Trim and discard mushroom stems. Dust inside of mushroom caps with cornstarch; shake to remove excess. Place a heaping tablespoon filling inside each mushroom cap.

3. Place a wide frying pan over low heat until hot. Add oil, swirling to coat sides. Add mushroom caps, half at a time, filling side down; cover and cook until golden brown, about 5 minutes.

In the past two decades, my love and enthusiasm for Asian cuisine are conveyed in many cooking classes and culinary conferences all over the world.

Makes 4 to 6 servings

Spareribs with Chayote

◆ Ingredients

5 dried black mushrooms

2 pieces tangerine peel

½ cup sliced pickled mustard greens

1 pound pork spareribs, cut into 2-inch pieces

2 medium-sized chayote

◆ Seasonings

1 cup chicken broth

1 cup water

2 tablespoons soy sauce

1 tablespoon dark soy sauce

1 tablespoon rice wine or dry sherry

¼ teaspoon salt

¼ teaspoon sugar

Cooking oil for deep-frying

6 cloves garlic

2 teaspoons minced garlic

1 green onion, cut into 1-½-inch pieces

2 teaspoons fermented black beans, rinsed

1 stalk lemongrass (bottom 6 inches only), lightly crushed and cut into 1-½-inch pieces

1 stick cinnamon

1 whole star anise

◆ Method

1. Place mushrooms, tangerine peel, and mustard greens in separate bowls and soak in warm water to cover until softened, about 15 minutes; drain. Trim and discard mushroom stems. Cut caps in half. Bring a saucepan of water to a boil over high heat. Add mustard greens and cook for 1 minute; drain.

2. Bring a pot of water to a boil over high heat. Add spareribs and parboil for 5 minutes. Pour into a colander and let drain.

3. Peel and seed chayote. Cut into 1-inch by 2-inch pieces; set aside.

4. Combine seasoning ingredients in a bowl; set aside.

5. Heat oil for deep-frying in a wok over high heat. Add whole garlic and deep-fry until golden brown, about 1 minute. Remove and drain on paper towels.

6. Remove all but 2 tablespoons oil from wok. Place wok over high heat until hot. Add minced garlic, green onion, and salted black beans; cook, stirring, until fragrant, about 10 seconds. Add spareribs and cook until lightly browned, about 1-½ minutes. Add mushrooms, tangerine peel, mustard greens, deep-fried garlic, lemongrass, cinnamon, and star anise; stir-fry for 2 minutes. Add seasonings and bring to a boil. Reduce heat to low, cover, and simmer for 40 minutes. Add chayote and continue cooking until tender, 8 to 10 minutes.

TIPS

When is a fruit not quite a fruit? When it's a chayote, for one. Also called a christophine or mirliton, this Central American fruit makes a great substitute for summer squash, green papaya, and similar gourd-like vegetables or bland-tasting fruits. Spot it by way of its pear shape and lumpy, pale green skin. Once you get it home, you'll find that its slightly sweet, starchy flesh, while edible raw, is best stewed, steamed, stir-fried, or otherwise given the standard vegetable treatment.

Makes 4 to 6 servings

Peking Sweet and Sour Pork

◆ Marinade

2 tablespoons soy sauce

1 tablespoon cornstarch

¼ teaspoon salt

1 pound boneless pork, cut into 1-inch pieces

1 cup all-purpose flour

◆ Seasonings

⅓ cup ketchup

¼ cup rice vinegar

3 tablespoons chicken broth

1 tablespoon soy sauce

2 teaspoons tomato paste

3 tablespoons packed brown sugar

Cooking oil for deep-frying

2 teaspoons minced ginger

⅓ cup diced onion

⅓ cup diced green bell pepper

⅓ cup diced red bell pepper

1 mango, peeled, seeded, and diced

1 green onion, cut into 1-½-inch pieces

◆ Method

1. Combine marinade ingredients in a bowl. Add pork and stir to coat. Let stand for 10 minutes. Coat pork with flour; shake to remove excess. Combine seasoning ingredients in a bowl; set aside.

2. Heat oil for deep-frying in a wok over high heat. Add pork and deep-fry until golden brown, about 3 minutes. Remove and drain on paper towels.

3. Remove all but 2 tablespoons oil from wok. Place wok over high heat until hot. Add ginger and onion; cook, stirring, until fragrant, about 10 seconds. Add green and red bell peppers; stir-fry for 30 seconds. Return pork to wok and add mango and green onion; stir-fry for 30 seconds. Add seasonings and cook until heated through.

"Yan Can Cook" enjoys popularity among viewers of all ages in over 70 countries around the world: the United States, Canada, and throughout Southeast Asia. Some of our loyal fans are children and it was great fun to invite them onto the show.

Makes 4 to 6 servings

Omelet Roll

◆ Marinade

1 tablespoon soy sauce

½ teaspoon cornstarch

¼ pound lean boneless pork, thinly sliced

◆ Omelet

8 eggs, lightly beaten

3 tablespoons water

½ teaspoon salt

◆ Seasonings

1 tablespoon hoisin sauce

1 tablespoon soy sauce

¼ teaspoon white pepper

4 tablespoons cooking oil

¼ pound fresh mung bean sprouts

¼ cup julienned cucumber

¼ cup thinly sliced cooked ham

2 yellow chives, cut into 2-inch pieces

½ red bell pepper, seeded and julienned

1 piece five-spice pressed bean curd, julienned

½ teaspoon cornstarch dissolved in 1 teaspoon water

◆ Method

1. Combine marinade ingredients in a bowl. Add pork and stir to coat. Let stand for 10 minutes. Combine omelet ingredients in a bowl; set aside. Combine seasoning ingredients in a bowl; set aside.

2. Place a wok over high heat until hot. Add 2 tablespoons oil, swirling to coat sides. Add pork and stir-fry for 1 minute. Add bean sprouts, cucumber, ham, chives, bell pepper, and bean curd; stir-fry for 30 seconds. Add seasonings and cook for 1 minute. Add cornstarch solution and cook, stirring, until sauce boils and thickens. Remove filling from wok and let cool.

3. To make each omelet: Place a non-stick omelet pan over medium-high heat until hot. Add 1 teaspoon oil, swirling to coat sides. Add ½ cup omelet mixture and cook without stirring. As edges begin to set, lift with a spatula and shake or tilt to let egg flow underneath. When egg no longer flows freely, turn omelet over and brown lightly on the other side. Slide omelet on a warm serving platter. Prepare remaining omelets with remaining egg mixture and oil.

4. To serve, place ¼ cup filling across center of a omelet. Fold long sides over filling and serve.

Makes 4 to 6 servings

TIPS

Do not wash eggs before storing them. There is a thin film on eggs which keeps micro-organisms from entering the eggs, so they will not spoil easily. Store eggs in the refrigerator for longer storage.

Hunan Spicy Tofu

◆Ingredients

1 package (16 ounces) soft tofu
1 tablespoon salted black beans

◆Seasonings

½ cup chicken broth
2 tablespoons dark soy sauce
1 teaspoon sesame oil
2 teaspoons sugar
¼ teaspoon Chinese five-spice

Cornstarch for dusting
Cooking oil for deep-frying
6 cloves garlic, sliced
2 jalapeño or serrano chiles, sliced
2 green onions, cut into 1-½-inch
    pieces
2 slices cooked ham, cut into 1-½-
    inch pieces
2 slices bacon, cut into 1-½-inch
    pieces
½ teaspoon cornstarch dissolved in
    1 teaspoon water

◆Method

1. Drain tofu and cut into 2-½-inch by 2-inch by 1-inch pieces. Soak black beans in warm water to cover for 5 minutes; drain and lightly crush. Combine seasoning ingredients in a bowl; set aside.

2. Heat oil for deep-frying in a wok over high heat. Dust tofu with cornstarch; shake to remove excess. Add tofu and deep-fry until golden brown, about 1 minute on each side. Remove and drain on paper towels.

3. Remove all but 2 tablespoons oil from wok. Place wok over high heat until hot. Add garlic, chiles, green onions, and black beans; cook, stirring, until fragrant, about 10 seconds. Add ham and bacon; stir-fry for 1 minute. Add tofu and seasonings; bring to a boil. Add cornstarch solution and cook, stirring, until sauce boils and thickens.

When in Rome, do as the Romans; and when in China, I kicked up my heels and danced in the streets of Beijing with these retirees.

Makes 4 to 6 servings

TIPS

If a Chinese recipe calls for salted black beans, don't just open the can of black beans with the highest sodium content you can find. Chinese salted black beans, preserved via fermentation and the addition of salt, are a very different ingredient altogether. These small, dark, and wrinkled beans have a pungent, smoky flavor that makes them common in all sorts of stir-fries and stews. To release their flavor, simply chop coarsely, mince, or crush with the end of the handle on your chef's knife. Whatever you do, you'll want to lightly rinse them before using to remove some of their salt. When choosing a plastic package of salted black beans, look for ones with firm, moist-looking beans; store the beans from an opened package in a tightly sealed container in a cool, dry place for up to a year.

Braised Stuffed Eggplant

◆ Ingredients

1 pound Asian eggplants

Cornstarch for dusting

◆ Filling

¼ cup chopped Sichuan preserved
   vegetable

½ pound lean boneless pork,
   chopped

1 egg, lightly beaten

1 tablespoon chopped green onion

1 tablespoon minced ginger

1 tablespoon chopped fresh Thai
   basil or cilantro

◆ Sauce

½ cup chicken broth

2 tablespoons white vinegar

1 tablespoon rice wine or dry
   sherry

1 tablespoon soy sauce

2 teaspoons sesame oil

2 teaspoons sugar

2 teaspoons cornstarch

2 tablespoons cooking oil

1 tablespoon minced garlic

1 teaspoon minced ginger

1 green onion, chopped

1 jalapeño or serrano chili, sliced

◆ Method

1. Cut eggplant diagonally into ½-inch thick slices. Cut each slice in half horizontally, but do not cut all the way through. Dust inside and outside with cornstarch; shake to remove excess. Let stand for 15 minutes.

2. Place filling ingredients in a food processor; process until smooth.

3. Combine sauce ingredients in a bowl; set aside.

4. To make each pocket: Place a heaping teaspoon pork filling in eggplant, smoothing sides, and gently pressing to form a sandwich. Dust with cornstarch; shake to remove excess.

5. Place a non-stick frying pan over high heat until hot. Add oil, swirling to coat sides. Add eggplant, half at a time, and pan-fry until golden brown, about 1-½ minutes on each side. Remove and drain on paper towels.

6. Reduce heat to medium-high. Add garlic, ginger, green onion, and chili; cook, stirring, until fragrant, about 10 seconds. Add sauce and bring to a boil. Reduce heat to medium-low. Add eggplant and simmer for 2 minutes.

Makes 4 to 6 servings

Rainbow Vegetables

◆ Ingredients

6 dried black mushrooms

◆ Sauce

¼ cup chicken broth or water

2 tablespoons soy sauce

1 tablespoon vegetarian oyster-flavored sauce

1-½ teaspoons fermented bean curd

½ teaspoon sugar

2 tablespoons cooking oil

2 teaspoons minced garlic

2 teaspoons minced ginger

½ cup baby corn, sliced in half diagonally

¼ cup sliced bamboo shoots

½ rib celery, thinly sliced diagonally

½ green bell pepper, seeded and cut into diamond shapes

½ red bell pepper, seeded and cut into diamond shapes

1 piece pressed bean curd, cut in half horizontally and cut into diamond shapes

1 green onion, cut into 2-inch pieces

½ teaspoon cornstarch dissolved in 1 teaspoon water

◆ Method

1. Soak mushrooms in warm water to cover until softened, about 15 minutes; drain. Trim and discard stems. Cut caps into quarters. Combine sauce ingredients in a bowl; set aside.

2. Place a wok over high heat until hot. Add oil, swirling to coat sides. Add garlic and ginger; cook, stirring, until fragrant, about 10 seconds. Add remaining ingredients, except sauce and cornstarch solution; stir-fry for 2 minutes. Add sauce and bring to a boil. Add cornstarch solution and cook, stirring, until sauce boils and thickens.

Since ancient times, bamboo has been a versatile material for countless household tools and kitchen utensils. And the young bamboo shoots are absolutely delicious in so many dishes.

Makes 4 to 6 servings

TIPS

The bean curd you see most often probably doesn't come in a jar. But that just may be because you're not familiar with fermented bean curd. Soft and creamy in texture, fermented bean curd comes in jars in small cubes with a mildly pungent, winey aroma. Some are whitish-beige in color, seasoned primarily with sesame oil and rice wine. On the other hand, the red-colored cubes of fermented bean curd get their flavor from red rice, rice wine, and chiles, and their color from annatto seeds. While a little bit of bean curd adds flavor and texture to sauces, both varieties are also delicious in stews and claypot casseroles, or even as a condiment served with other dishes.

Pei-Pa Tofu

◆ Tofu Mixture

1 package (16 ounces) firm tofu

4 dried black mushrooms

2 tablespoons chopped Sichuan preserved vegetable

¼ cup chopped water chestnuts

3 tablespoons chopped bamboo shoots

2 tablespoons chopped cooked ham

1 tablespoon chopped cilantro

1 green onion, chopped

1 egg, lightly beaten

2 tablespoons cornstarch

1 teaspoon sesame oil

½ teaspoon onion salt

¼ teaspoon white pepper

Cooking oil for brushing

◆ Sauce

½ cup chicken broth

1 tablespoon oyster-flavored sauce

1 tablespoon soy sauce

1 tablespoon cornstarch

2 tablespoons cooking oil

Cilantro sprigs for garnish

◆ Method

1. Drain and mash tofu. Let stand for 10 minutes. Remove excess liquid. Soak mushrooms in warm water to cover until softened, about 15 minutes. Trim and discard stems. Chop caps.

2. Place tofu in a bowl and add mushrooms and remaining tofu mixture ingredients; mix well.

3. Prepare a wok for steaming. Lightly brush the insides of 15 Chinese soup spoons with oil. Fill each spoon with about 1-½ tablespoons tofu mixture, shaping and smoothing sides. Place filled spoons in wok and steam until firm, 5 to 6 minutes. Carefully remove steamed tofu from spoons.

4. Combine sauce ingredients in a saucepan. Bring to a boil over high heat. Reduce heat to low and cook until slightly thickened.

5. Place a non-stick frying pan over medium-high heat until hot. Add oil, swirling to coat sides. Add steamed tofu and pan-fry, turning once, until light brown, about 1 minute on each side.

6. Arrange tofu pillows on a serving platter. Pour sauce over tofu pillows and garnish with cilantro sprigs.

Makes 4 to 6 servings

Pumpkin Stew

◆ Ingredients

2 tablespoons dried wolfberries (optional)

¾ pound pumpkin

◆ Seasonings

⅔ cup chicken broth or water

2 tablespoons evaporated milk

2 teaspoons rice wine or dry sherry

2 teaspoons sesame oil

½ teaspoon salt

½ teaspoon sugar

¼ teaspoon white pepper

Cooking oil for deep-frying

1 tablespoon diced cooked ham

2 green onions, cut into 2-inch pieces

¼ cup sliced bamboo shoots

◆ Method

1. Soak wolfberries in warm water to cover until softened, about 15 minutes; drain. Peel and seed pumpkin. Cut pumpkin into 1-inch pieces. Combine seasoning ingredients in a bowl; set aside.

2. Heat oil for deep-frying in a wok over high heat. Add pumpkin and deep-fry for 2 minutes. Remove and drain on paper towels.

3. Place a pot over high heat until hot. Add 1 tablespoon oil, swirling to coat sides. Add ham and cook, stirring, until fragrant, about 10 seconds. Add pumpkin, wolfberries, and green onions; stir-fry for 2 minutes. Add bamboo shoots and seasonings; bring to a boil. Reduce heat to medium, cover, and cook until pumpkin is tender, about 5 minutes.

TIPS

Wolfberries are the seeds of the vegetable, Chinese Box Thorn. The Hubei province in China produces the best quality wolfberries. Chinese herbalists believe wolfberries are good for the eyes and complexion.

Makes 4 to 6 servings

Noodle-Vegetable Soup

◆ Seasonings

2 tablespoons rice wine or dry sherry

1 tablespoon vegetarian oyster-flavored sauce

1 teaspoon sesame oil

½ teaspoon sugar

¼ teaspoon white pepper

¼ pound napa cabbage, sliced

2 cups chicken broth or water

1 tablespoon julienned Sichuan preserved vegetable

1 green onion, cut into 2-inch pieces

¼ cup julienned bamboo shoots

2 tablespoons julienned cooked ham

2 ounces dried bean thread noodles

2 yellow chives, cut into 2-inch pieces

◆ Method

1. Combine seasoning ingredients in a bowl; set aside.

2. Bring a pot of water to a boil over high heat. Add napa cabbage and cook for 1 minute; drain.

3. Place cabbage at bottom of a clay pot. Add chicken broth and bring to a boil over medium heat. Add preserved vegetable, green onion, bamboo shoots, ham, and seasonings; cook for 3 minutes. Add bean thread noodles and cook until noodles soften, 2 to 3 minutes. Add yellow chives and mix well.

Makes 4 to 6 servings

Hot and Sour Chicken Soup

◆ Ingredients

10 dried wood ears

¼ pound boneless, skinless chicken

◆ Marinade

1 teaspoon soy sauce

½ teaspoon cornstarch

◆ Seasonings

¼ cup black vinegar

1 tablespoon soy sauce

1 tablespoon dark soy sauce

½ teaspoon sugar

◆ Dough

1 cup hot water

1 cup glutinous rice flour

4 cups chicken broth

¼ cup julienned bamboo shoots

⅓ cup julienned carrot

2 slices ginger, julienned

1 jalapeño or serrano chili, seeded and thinly sliced

1 green onion, sliced

1 tablespoon cornstarch dissolved in 2 tablespoons water

◆ Method

1. Soak wood ears in warm water to cover until softened, about 15 minutes; drain. Thinly slice wood ears; set aside. Cut chicken into thin slices then cut each slice into thin strips. Place chicken in a bowl and add marinade ingredients; stir to coat. Let stand for 10 minutes. Combine seasoning ingredients in a bowl; set aside.

2. Add hot water to flow in a bowl and mix until dough comes together. Remove dough to a floured surface and knead until smooth. Roll dough into a cylinder, about ½-inch in diameter. Cut dough into ½-inch pieces. Roll each piece into a ball.

3. Place broth in a pot and bring to a boil over high heat. Add wood ear, chicken, bamboo shoots, carrot, ginger, chili, and seasonings; bring to a boil. Reduce heat to low and simmer for 2 minutes. Add dough balls and green onion; cook for 3 minutes. Add cornstarch solution and cook, stirring, until soup thickens.

This is probably the biggest Mongolian hot-pot in the world. They say that it can feed a thousand people, I think it can probably bathe a few hundred...

Makes 4 to 6 servings

Seafood-Tofu Soup

◆ Ingredients

¼ cup small raw shrimp

⅓ cup bay scallops

◆ Marinade

½ teaspoon cornstarch

¼ teaspoon salt

¼ teaspoon white pepper

½ package (about 7 ounces) soft tofu

1 tablespoon cooking oil

2 slices ginger, julienned

4 cups chicken broth

1-½ tablespoons chopped Sichuan preserved vegetable

1 tomato, seeded and diced

1 slice lemon

½ cup straw mushrooms

2 tablespoon frozen green peas, thawed

1 teaspoon garlic chives, cut into 1-inch pieces

2 teaspoons soy sauce

1 teaspoon sesame oil

2-½ tablespoons cornstarch dissolved in 3 tablespoons water

1 egg white, lightly beaten

◆ Method

1. Shell and devein shrimp. Place shrimp and scallops in a bowl and add scallops. Add marinade ingredients and mix well. Let stand for 10 minutes.

2. Drain tofu and cut into ½-inch cubes; set aside.

3. Place a wok over high heat until hot. Add oil, swirling to coat sides. Add ginger and cook, stirring, until fragrant, about 10 seconds. Add shrimp and scallops; stir-fry for 1 minute. Add chicken broth and bring to a boil. Add preserved vegetable, tofu, tomato, lemon, straw mushrooms, peas, chives, soy sauce, and sesame oil; cook for 2 minutes. Add cornstarch solution and cook, stirring, until soup thickens. Turn off heat. Add egg white, stirring, until it forms long threads.

Makes 4 to 6 servings

TIPS

When thickening sauces, add tapioca starch solution slowly, cook over medium to high heat, and stir constantly to prevent lumps from forming. Cornstarch or potato starch can also be used to thicken sauces.

Savory Fish Soup

◆ Marinade

1 teaspoon soy sauce

½ teaspoon cornstarch

¼ teaspoon salt

¼ teaspoon white pepper

¼ pound firm white fish fillet, such as sea bass or red snapper, sliced

2 tablespoons dried wolfberries

2-½ cups chicken broth

2 slices ginger, lightly crushed

2 fresh shiitake mushrooms, trimmed and sliced

¼ cup straw mushrooms

2 tablespoons rice wine or dry sherry

1-½ tablespoons fresh enoki mushrooms, trimmed

1 green onion, cut into 1-½-inch pieces

Salt, white pepper, and sesame oil to taste

◆ Method

1. Combine marinade ingredients in a bowl. Add fish and stir to coat. Let stand for 10 minutes. Soak wolfberries in warm water to cover until softened, about 15 minutes; drain.

2. Place broth in a pot and bring to a boil over high heat. Add wolfberries, ginger, shiitake mushrooms, straw mushrooms, and rice wine; cook for 2 minutes. Add fish and cook for 1 minute. Add enoki mushrooms and green onion; cook for 30 seconds. Season with salt, white pepper, and sesame oil to taste.

Makes 4 to 6 servings

TIPS

Making fish soup: Before adding the fish, first bring water to a boil so soup won't taste fishy. Pan-frying fish before adding to water makes the soup milky white.

Chicken Congee

◆ Ingredients

½ cup uncooked long-grain rice
1 tablespoon cooking oil
½ teaspoon salt
6 cups chicken broth
3 cups water

½ pound boneless, skinless chicken
2 ounces small squid, cleaned

◆ Marinade

1 teaspoon soy sauce
1 teaspoon cornstarch
¼ teaspoon salt
¼ teaspoon white pepper

2 slices ginger, julienned
4 to 6 eggs
½ green onion, sliced
2 Chinese doughnuts, sliced, or
   similar long, tubular piece of
   fried dough
Salt and white pepper to taste

◆ Method

1. Wash and drain rice. Place rice in a bowl and add oil and salt; mix well. Let stand for 10 minutes.

2. Place rice in a pot and add chicken broth and water. Bring to a boil over high heat. Reduce heat to medium-high. Cook, stirring occasionally, for 5 minutes. Reduce heat to low and simmer, stirring occasionally, for 1-½ to 2 hours.

3. Thinly slice chicken then cut slices into thin strips. Separate squid tentacles from body. Slice open squid hoods and lightly score them diagonally with crosshatching marks ½ inch apart. Cut body into thin strips. Leave tentacles whole. Place chicken and squid in a bowl. Add marinade ingredients and mix well. Let stand for 10 minutes.

4. Bring a pot of water to a boil over high heat. Add chicken and squid; cook for 1 minute. Pour into a colander and let drain.

5. Add chicken, squid, and ginger to congee. Cook for 2 minutes.

6. Ladle congee into individual soup bowls. Crack egg over congee. Sprinkle green onion over congee and serve with doughnut slices on the side. Season with salt and white pepper to taste.

Rice grown the old fashion way is labor-intensive and back-breaking. Here I am lending a land, or maybe I should say, a back...

Makes 4 to 6 servings

Pasta with Seafood Sauce

◆ Ingredients

¼ pound medium raw prawns

¼ pound firm white fish fillet, such as sea bass or red snapper

¼ cup bay scallops

◆ Marinade

1 tablespoon white wine

½ teaspoon salt

¼ teaspoon white pepper

½ pound dried pasta, such as spaghetti, fettucine, or linguine

1 teaspoon sesame oil

2 tablespoons cooking oil

1 teaspoon minced garlic

4 black olives, pitted and diced

¼ green bell pepper, seeded and diced

1-½ cups prepared tomato basil pasta sauce

◆ Method

1. Shell and devein prawns. Dice prawns. Cut fish into small pieces. Place prawns, fish, and scallops in a bowl. Add marinade ingredients and stir to coat. Let stand for 10 minutes.

2. Bring a pot of water to a boil over high heat. Add pasta and cook according to package directions. Drain, rinse with cold water, and drain again. Place noodles in a serving platter and add sesame oil; toss to coat.

3. Place a wok over high heat until hot. Add oil, swirling to coat sides. Add garlic and olives; cook, stirring, until fragrant, about 10 seconds. Add seafood and bell peppers; stir-fry for 2 minutes. Add pasta sauce and bring to a boil. Pour seafood mixture over pasta and serve.

Culinary experts all over the world are most gracious in sharing their culinary talents and skills.

Makes 4 to 6 servings

TIPS

During the 13th century, Marco Polo brought spaghetti to Italy after his visit to China. Cook spaghetti in a big pot of boiling salted water until al dente. Drain and rinse under cold running water to stop the cooking process. Traditionally, in Italy, cooked spaghetti is drained, the sauce is added, and it is served immediately.

Chinese-style Pizza

◆ Dough

1 cup warm water

2-¼ teaspoons dry active yeast

2-½ to 3 cups all-purpose flour

¾ teaspoon salt

¼ teaspoon sugar

◆ Sauce

⅓ cup tomato sauce

¼ cup tomato paste

1 tablespoon hoisin sauce

1 teaspoon sesame paste

½ teaspoon chili garlic sauce

¼ teaspoon salt

◆ Toppings

1-½ cups shredded mozzarella cheese

½ cup shredded cooked chicken

6 white button mushrooms, trimmed and sliced

2 green onions, thinly sliced

½ green bell pepper, seeded and sliced

½ Chinese sausage, sliced

1 tablespoon chopped anchovies (optional)

◆ Method

1. To make dough: Pour water in a bowl. Sprinkle yeast over water and stir until dissolved. Let stand until small bubbles form, about 10 minutes. Place flour, salt, and sugar in a bowl; mix well. Add yeast and mix well. Place dough on a lightly floured surface and knead until smooth and elastic, about 5 minutes. Place dough in a lightly greased bowl; turn to coat. Cover with a dry cloth. Let rise in a warm area until dough doubles in bulk, about 1 hour. Punch dough down and roll out to form a 12-inch circle. Transfer dough to a greased pizza pan.

2. Combine sauce ingredients in a bowl and mix well. Spread sauce over dough. Sprinkle toppings over sauce.

3. Preheat oven to 425°F. Bake pizza until crust is golden brown and cheese has melted, 15 to 20 minutes.

TIPS

If you really want to give this pizza a Chinese spin, be sure to use Chinese sausages: small, wrinkled, sweet-savory links with a dark reddish-brown color and dry outer texture. Inside that bumpy exterior is a filling made from pork, duck, or beef seasoned with salt, sugar, and rice wine. In addition to serving as unbeatable pizza toppings, these little sausages are great chopped for dumpling fillings, sliced and tossed into stir-fried or steamed rice dishes, or even nibbled on their own. Be sure to fully cook them before eating, and store Chinese sausages in a tightly sealed container in the refrigerator.

Makes 4 to 6 servings

Chilled Lychees and Snow Fungus

◆Ingredients

½ ounce dried snow fungus

¼ pound cantaloupe, seeded

¼ pound plums, pitted

5 cups water

⅓ cup rock sugar

1 cup lychees

1 egg white, lightly beaten

◆Method

1. Soak snow fungus in warm water to cover until softened, about 5 minutes. Drain and tear into bite-size pieces. Cut cantaloupe and plums into bite-size pieces.

2. Place water in a pot and bring to a boil over high heat. Add rock sugar and cook until sugar dissolves, about 5 minutes. Add cantaloupe, plums, and lychees; bring to a boil. Reduce heat to low. Simmer for 3 minutes. Turn off heat. Add egg white, stirring, until it forms long threads. Serve hot or cold.

TIPS

Snow fungus may not be the first thing you think of when it's time for dessert, but don't let the name of this dried, golden-beige to cream-colored, spongy-looking delicacy fool you: its crunchy texture turns to a luscious, gelatinous smoothness as it cooks, and since it has no real flavor of its own, it easily absorbs those of other ingredients paired with it. Hence, its popularity in desserts such as sweet soups and this fruit-and-fungus combination. And that the cooked fungus turns a gleaming silvery-white after cooking makes it a striking way to end a meal as well. Make sure to soak snow fungus before cooking, but keep in mind that they grow in volume many times over their dried size. You'll find white fungus in plastic bags or boxes of twelve; store the pieces in a tightly sealed container in a cool, dry place for several months.

Makes 4 to 6 servings

◆ Pastry Cream

1 tablespoon butter
½ egg yolk
¼ cup sugar

1 cup diced strawberries
⅔ cup diced mangoes
2 kiwifruit, peeled and diced
9 spring roll wrappers
Cooking oil for deep-frying

◆ Method

1. Combine pastry cream ingredients in a bowl. Blend until smooth. Add strawberries, mangoes, and kiwifruit; mix well.

2. To make each roll: Place ⅓ cup fruit mixture along center of a spring roll wrapper. Fold left and right ends over filling then roll up to form a cylinder. Seal with a flour paste.

3. Heat oil for deep-frying in a wok over high heat until hot. Add rolls, 3 at a time, and deep-fry until golden brown, 2 to 3 minutes. Remove and drain on paper towels.

Fruit-filled Spring Rolls

Makes 9 rolls

Eight Treasure Rice Pudding

◆ Ingredients

2 cups uncooked glutinous rice, rinsed and drained

3 cups water

1 tablespoon cooking oil

¼ cup sugar

◆ Cooking oil for brushing

10 candied lotus seeds

6 candied red dates

4 maraschino cherries, cut in half

3 dried apricots, cut into quarters

2 candied kumquats, sliced

2 tablespoons dried cherries

2 tablespoons raisins

1 cup lotus seed paste

◆ Syrup

½ cup water

1 tablespoon lemon juice

1 cup sugar

2 teaspoons cornstarch dissolved in 1 tablespoon water

◆ Method

1. Soak rice in water to cover for 2 hours; drain. Combine rice and water in a saucepan; bring to a boil over medium-high heat. Cook, uncovered, until crater-like holes appear, about 10 minutes. Reduce heat to low. Cover and cook for 15 to 20 minutes. Remove rice to a bowl and add oil and sugar; mix well.

2. Brush oil on bottoms and sides of two 1-quart glass bowls. Arrange half of lotus seeds, red dates, maraschino cherries, apricots, kumquats, cherries, and raisins in a pattern over bottom of each bowl. Carefully spread one-fourth of rice over each fruit arrangement. Press rice down gently. Spread ½ cup lotus seed paste over each layer of rice. Spread half of remaining rice over lotus seed paste. Press rice down gently. Cover each bowl with a damp cloth.

3. Prepare a wok for steaming. Place filled bowls in wok and steam for 30 minutes.

4. Combine syrup ingredients in a saucepan. Bring to a boil over high heat. Add cornstarch solution and cook, stirring, until sauce boils and thickens. Reduce heat to low and keep warm.

5. Remove bowls from steamer. Cover mold with a serving platter and invert, gently shaking to unmold. Pour hot syrup over pudding and serve.

To get the freshest ingredients we must get to the source, even if it means perfecting my climbing skills...

Makes 4 to 6 servings

Sweet Tapioca with Melon

◆ Ingredients

2 tablespoons small (⅛-inch)
   pearl tapioca

4 cups water

½ cup sugar

1 cup finely diced cantaloupe

1 cup finely diced honeydew
   melon

◆ Method

1. Soak tapioca in cold water to cover for 10 minutes (most of water will be absorbed); drain.

2. Place water in a saucepan and bring to a boil over high heat. Reduce heat to low. Add tapioca and sugar; cook, stirring occasionally, until tapioca becomes translucent, 8 to 10 minutes. Remove tapioca from heat and let cool. Add cantaloupe and honeydew melons; mix well. Cover and refrigerate until chilled.

Makes 4 to 6 servings

TIPS

From the tips of its leaves and flowers all the way down to its roots, the lotus plant is firmly rooted in Chinese culture, so to speak. And that helps sow the seeds for some creatively delicious additions to Chinese cuisine as well, not the least of which are lotus seeds themselves. Inventive Chinese cooks have developed all sorts of ways to use these delicately flavored seeds. You can find them fresh, dried, and canned for use in savory stuffings and stews, and even candied for use in desserts–Eight Treasure Rice Pudding being a common example. A thick, sweet paste of cooked, ground, and sweetened lotus seeds makes a classic filling for steamed and baked buns, the perfect endings to any dim sum brunch.

Poached Pears in Red Wine

◆Ingredients
3 kiwifruit
3 pears

◆Poaching Liquid
3 cups red wine
½ cup water
½ cup sugar
2 tablespoons black tea leaves
4 whole cloves
1 stick cinnamon

3 tablespoons sugar
1 tablespoon cornstarch dissolved in 2 tablespoons water

◆Method

1. Peel kiwifruit and place in a food processor. Puree until smooth; set aside.

2. Peel pears; remove cores with a melon baller. Place pears in a bowl and cover with water to prevent browning.

3. Combine poaching liquid ingredients in a saucepan. Bring to a boil over high heat. Drain pears and add to poaching liquid; bring to a boil. Reduce heat to low. Simmer until pears are barely tender, about 30 minutes. Remove pears and reserve poaching liquid.

4. Place 1 cup reserved poaching liquid in a saucepan. Add kiwifruit puree and sugar; bring to a boil. Add cornstarch solution and cook, stirring, until sauce boils and thickens.

5. To serve: Spoon sauce onto a dessert plate. Cut pears in half. Slice pear half but do not cut through to stem. Gently fan pear slices and place over sauce.

Makes 4 to 6 servings

Bean curd sheets: by products of bean curd processing; brittle skins formed atop vats of bean curd, removed as sheets and dried; soak to soften and use as wrapper for fillings, or add to steamed, stir-fried, and braised dishes; crumble into soups and stews

Bean curd sticks: sheets of bean curd skin that are crumpled into long, slender, brittle sticks; once soaked in warm water, have chewy, meat-like texture and bland flavor; great for absorbing flavors of rich sauces, gravies, and stews

Bean thread noodles: dried noodles made from mung bean starch (also called cellophane noodles); before using, soak in warm water until softened

Black mushrooms (dried): open-capped mushrooms with brownish-black caps and tan gills; firm and chewy in texture, with meaty flavor that intensifies when dried; use sliced in stir-fries or chopped in dumpling fillings

Chili garlic sauce: made from blend of fresh and dried chiles, vinegar, and often garlic, fermented black beans, sesame oil, and spices; use in sauces and stir-fries for spicy, flavorful bite

Chinese five-spice: Powder cocoa-colored powder made from cinnamon, cloves, fennel, Sichuan peppercorns, and star anise; adds sweet and spicy flavor to marinades, sauces, braised, and red-cooked dishes

Daikon: long, slender Japanese radish with crisp, white flesh and peppery taste; peeled and shredded for use as sushi garnish in Japan; enjoyed in stews and braised dishes in China; substitute potato or turnip if daikon is unavailable

Dark soy sauce: regular soy sauce with molasses added for darker color, thicker consistency, and slight sweetness; gives mahogany color and rich flavor to dips, sauces, stir-fries, and red-cooked dishes

Dried shrimp: small, dried, and brine-preserved shrimp; chewy, highly flavored ingredients in soups and dumpling fillings; make tasty snacks on their own

Enoki mushrooms: pale ivory, long-stemmed fresh mushrooms with tiny caps and delicate flavor; use in soups or salads, or as garnish

Five-spice pressed bean curd: firm, compact, reddish-brown bean curd which has been drained of most of its whey, marinated, and sold in flat cakes; use in stews, salads, stir-fries, and vegetarian dishes

Garlic chives, yellow chives: also called Chinese chives; similar to Western chives but with distinct garlic flavor and aroma; can find long, green, grass-like varieties; shorter, tender, yellow kinds; and green flowering types with edible blossoms; available seasonably in spring and summer; use in soups and stir-fries and as garnish

Glutinous rice: short-grain rice also known as sweet or sticky rice; grains small and pearl-shaped; high starch content contributes to soft texture and stickiness perfect for puddings and desserts

Longans: oval fruit with smooth brown shell; taste similar to lychees but are slightly smaller; available in cans and occasionally fresh; excellent in fruit salads or as snack

Lychees: small, round sweet fruit with juicy, pearly white flesh; fresh fruit has bumpy reddish-pink skin removed before canning; usually available canned in syrup

Pearl tapioca: tapioca starch processed into pellets ranging in size from small seeds to peas; used to thicken sauces and make creamy, pearly-textured pudding and desserts

Rice wine: amber-colored liquid made from fermented glutinous rice and millet; aged 10 to 100 years; Shao Hsing, in eastern China, known for high-quality rice wines; common ingredient in sauces and marinades; substitute dry sherry if rice wine is unavailable

Sesame paste: toasted white sesame seeds ground into thick paste with roasted, nutty aroma and flavor; common in Sichuan dishes and nutty sauces

Shiitake mushrooms: similar to black mushrooms in color, texture and flavor; available fresh as well as dried; use in same manner as dried black mushrooms

Sichuan preserved vegetable: dark-green and spicy-salty kohlrabi, mustard greens, napa cabbage, or turnips, preserved with chile powder and Sichuan peppercorns; finely chop for dumpling fillings or coarsely chop for soups and stews

Star anise: small, inedible, star-shaped pod with shiny reddish seed in each of eight points; adds distinct licorice flavor to stews, sauces, and braised dishes, removed after cooking

Tangerine peel (dried): wrinkled, dark-orange dried peel used to flavor soups, stews, and sauces; soak to soften and scrape off bitter white layer under peel before using

Taro root: dark- and rough-skinned root with starchy, purple-grey flesh and slightly sweet, nutty flavor; comes in wide range of sizes; use in same manner as potato, peeling first before boiling, steaming, shredding, or mashing; add to soups and stews for texture

Thai basil: pungent, slightly minty herb; has longer, narrower pale green leaves than Western sweet basil; sometimes called holy basil; if unavailable, substitute sweet basil

Wood ears (dried): variety of dried black fungus with dark, leathery appearance; chewy in texture and bland in flavor when soaked to soften in warm water